Perfect

Words and music by Ed Sheeran

Arranged for lever or pedal harp by Sylvia Woods

Sylvia Woods has included two harp arrangements of Ed Sheeran's *Perfect* in this folio. Both versions can be played on either lever harp or pedal harp.

The first arrangement (pages 1 through 6) is the complete piece.

The shorter, two-page version on pages 7 and 8 includes only the first verse. It is exactly the same as the first 52 measures of the complete version, with a short ending added. This version is perfect for wedding processionals, and other occasions when your playing time is limited, and you don't want to worry about turning pages.

The low D in the left hand of measure 16 in both versions may be omitted if you do not have that string on your harp.

1

Perfect
(complete arrangement)

Repeated melody notes with no fingerings
may be played with finger 1, 2 or 3.

Words and music by ED SHEERAN
Arranged for harp by SYLVIA WOODS

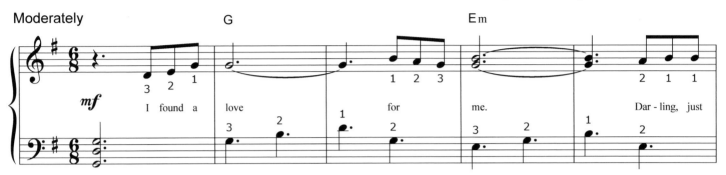

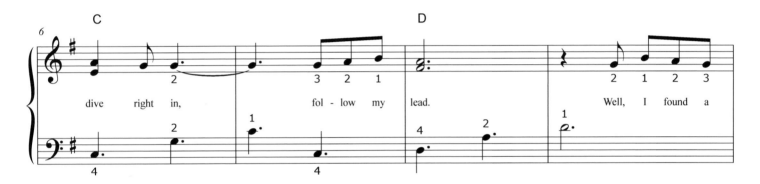

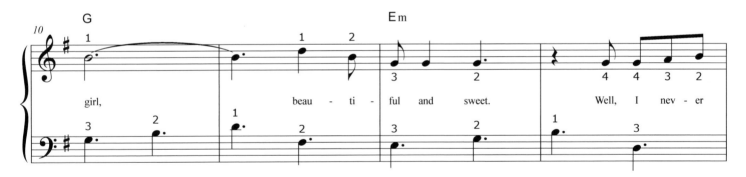

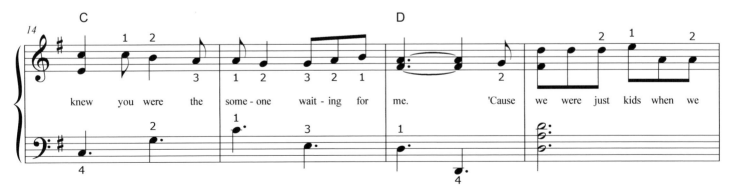

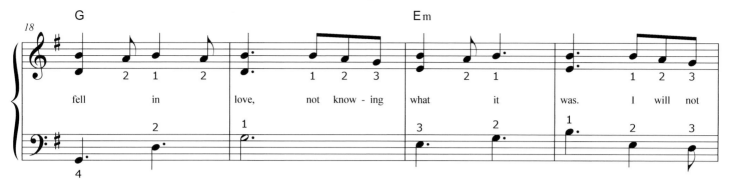

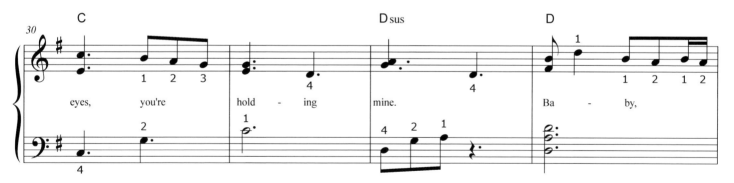

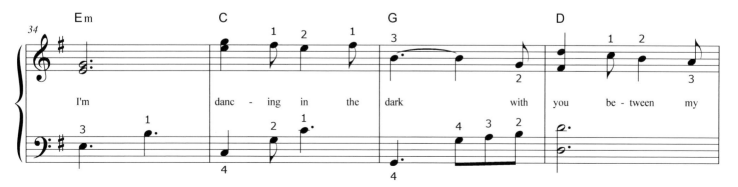

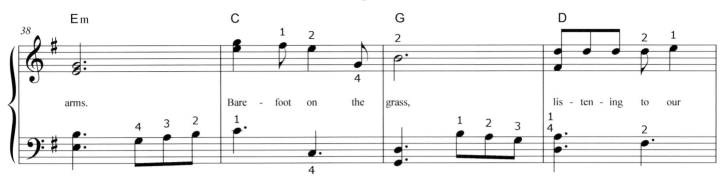

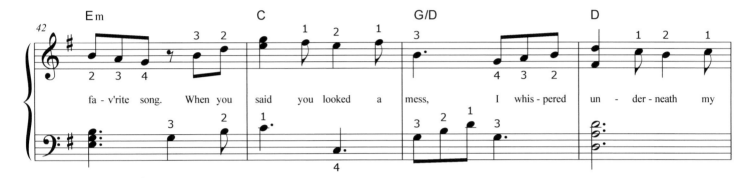

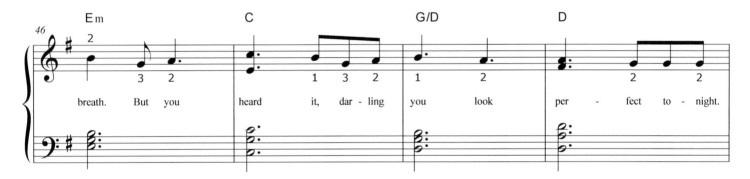

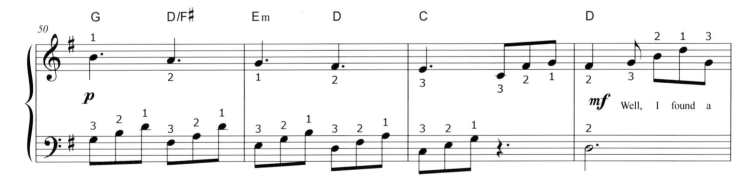

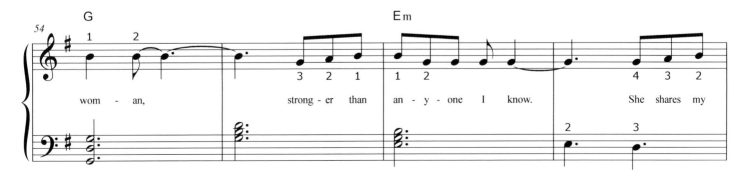

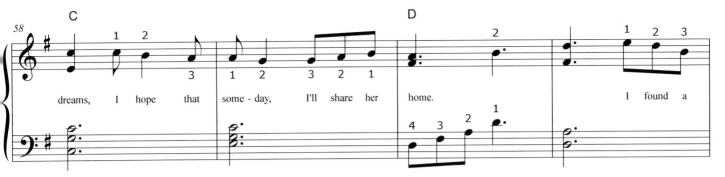

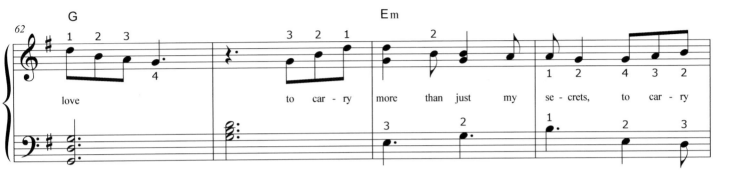

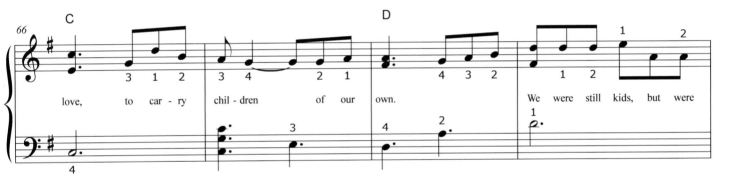

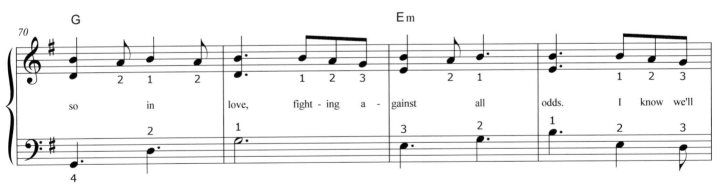

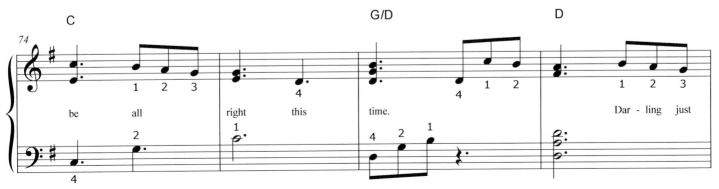

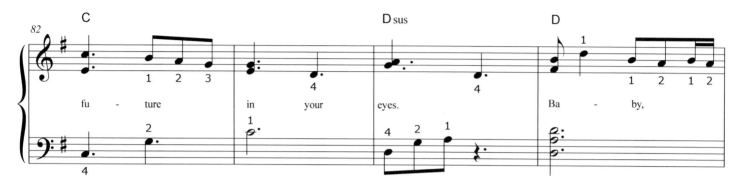

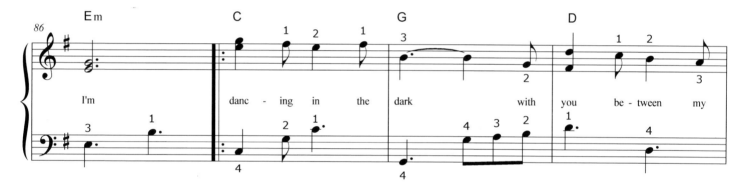

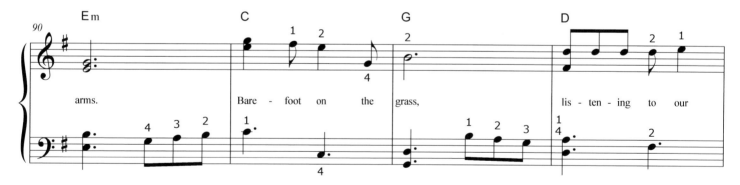

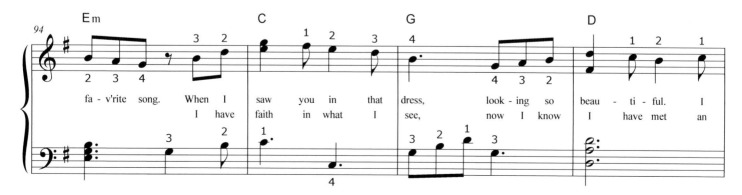

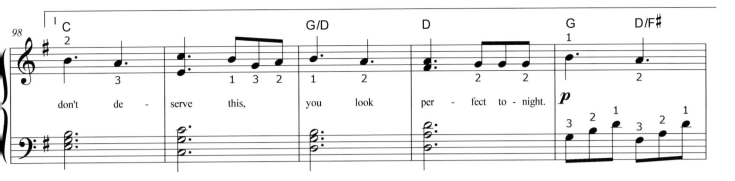

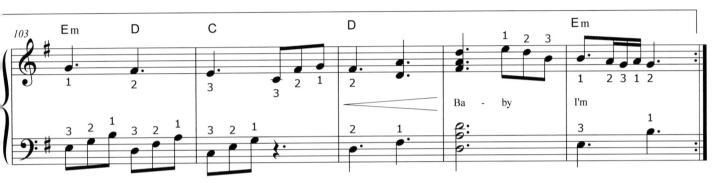

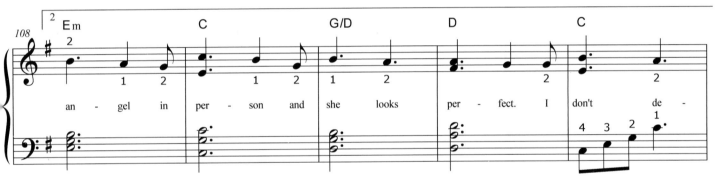

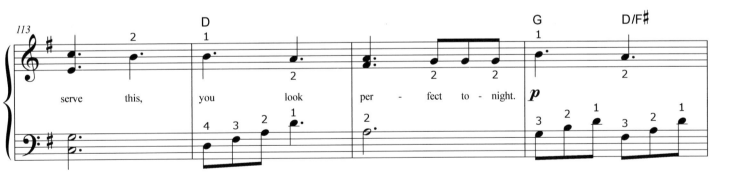

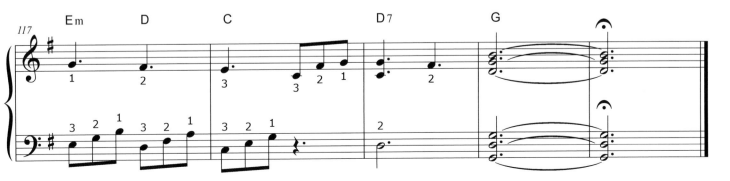

Perfect
(2-page, 1-verse arrangement)

Repeated melody notes with no fingerings may be played with finger 1, 2 or 3.

Words and music by ED SHEERAN
Arranged for harp by SYLVIA WOODS